Spiritual Exercises
for Church Leaders

Participant's Book

Spiritual Exercises for Church Leaders

Dolores R. Leckey
and
Paula Minaert

Participant's Book

A Project of the
Woodstock Theological Center

PAULIST PRESS
New York • Mahwah, N.J.

Cover design by Valerie Petro

Book design by ediType

Illustrations copyright © 2003 by Stephen Titra

Copyright © 2003 by The Woodstock Theological Center

Library of Congress Cataloging-in-Publication Data

Leckey, Dolores R.
    Spiritual exercises for church leaders : participant's book / Dolores R. Leckey, Paula Minaert.
        p. cm.
    "A project of the Woodstock Theological Center."
    Includes bibliographical references.
    ISBN 0-8091-4163-9
    1. Christian leadership–Catholic Church. 2. Spiritual exercises. I. Minaert, Paula. II. Title.
    BX1803 .L432 2003
    248.8'9–dc21

                                                                        2002156413

Published by Paulist Press
997 Macarthur Boulevard
Mahwah, New Jersey 07430

www.paulistpress.com

Printed and bound in the
United States of America

Contents

Foreword

Spirituality —
A Pearl of Great Price

In his classic *Markings,* Dag Hammarskjöld (1905–1961), former secretary general of the United Nations, expressed a deep spiritual longing: "If only I may grow: firmer, simpler — quieter, warmer."[1]

Hammarskjöld was a political leader, one who served the common good and fostered world peace. In his spiritual journal he records little of his political involvement but centers on his relationship with God and how that relationship impacted the rest of his life. Journaling was for him a spiritual exercise of utmost importance, fostering a sense of clarity, depth, and continuity.

All of us who are called to be leaders — be it in the Church, our homes, or society at large, have a need to grow firmer in our convictions, simpler in our lifestyle, quieter in the interior of our hearts, warmer in our relationships. We grow through exercising our spiritual faculties of knowing and loving, of imaging and remembering, of pondering and deciding. In *Spiritual Exercises for Church Leaders* we are given a vision and a methodology for ongoing personal and communal development. This work incorporates the insights and practical wisdom of two great teachers: St. Ignatius of Loyola and Bernard Lonergan. Here is a book that takes us into the mystery of the human person and offers ways in which we might

7

live more effectively the call to be truly human, truly disciples of the Lord Jesus.

Spirituality is about growth, developing our potential in reference to God and how that life in God impacts all the other aspects of our life: the social, the political, the cultural, the economic. Three major calls comprise our spiritual journey: the call to listen attentively, the call to respond wholeheartedly, the call to participate fully.

To listen attentively. The French philosopher Simone Weil held the conviction that *attention* is central both to a Christian conception of studies and the command to love. She writes: "Not only does the love of God have attention for its substance; the love of our neighbor, which we know to be the same love, is made of this same substance."[2] In an age suffering from the malady of inattentiveness, our challenge is to be open to the divine speech. God speaks to us through everyday experiences, the intuitions of the heart, the legacy of our rich Christian tradition, the Bible. Two requirements on our part: a radical openness and a deep interior silence. To be human is to hear. Other voices seek our attention: the radio and television, the roar of the madding crowd, our own interior Grand Central Station. The din and cacophony can be overwhelming. Yet God not only speaks to us but offers the Holy Spirit to dwell within us to help us discern the action of divine grace. With Jesus as mentor and model we have a message and a lifestyle that help us to sort out what is of God — light, love, life — and what is not — darkness, indifference, and death.

To respond wholeheartedly. Listening is one side of the coin, loving is the other. The Carmelite poet Jessica Powers maintained that to live with the Spirit of God embraced two things: being a listener and being a lover. Our hearing of God's word — to feed the hungry, to forgive sins seventy times seven times, to carry one another's burdens — is to be followed by a wholehearted response. Nonresponsiveness, like inattentiveness, is death to spirituality.

St. Thérèse of Lisieux, affectionately known as the Little Flower, was a responder to God's call. She saw her vocation as a call to love, to be love, to make Love loved. Though she lived only twenty-four years, she lived a full life. This Doctor of the Church models for us someone who lived intensely the Ignatian process of loving attention, one who explored and discerned, one who acted with great responsibility, one who treasured not only her own community but through missionary zeal, the whole Church.

To participate fully. An old adage: "Growth demands participation." We are not here on earth to be observers, watching life pass us by. We are to enter in, tasting the joys and sorrows of life, experiencing victories and defeats, sharing good and tough times. Spirituality is a full participation in the paschal mystery.

Robert Ellsberg, in his book *All Saints,* gives a brief summary of the life and ministry of 365 individuals who refused the role of observer and committed themselves to participate fully in the vocation God assigned to them. We are told about the great saints such as Augustine of Hippo and Teresa of Avila; we hear about the Hindu "saint" Gandhi, who led his country to freedom and independence; we are shown the dedication of Dorothy Day and her Catholic Worker movement as well as Dietrich Bonhoeffer, who boldly stated the cost of discipleship. These people, all leaders in their various areas, emphasized the importance of spiritual discipline if they were to grow in justice and holiness. Listening, exploring, discerning, responding — markings that led them and their people to fullness of life.

Spiritual Exercises for Church Leaders is theological and practical. It offers a perspective on human existence and a methodology proven in its development of human potential. Its value lies in its participatory style, its clarity of purpose, its realism. While highly pragmatic, it also contains a depth that leads to transformation.

In the Second Vatican Council document *Lumen Gentium,* the Dogmatic Constitution on the Church, we are reminded that our universal call is to holiness. Our vocation is to sanctity. *Spiritual Exercises for Church Leaders* is intended to be a helpful resource in responding to the call. It is clear from the text that our response is both a matter of grace and serious human work. Further, this call to holiness is neither romantic nor remote. The poet Gordon Gilsdorf captures well the essence of sanctity:

A SAINT

We look
for mystic gold
and silvered ecstasy
and find a tempered, twisted piece
of steel.[3]

Robert F. Morneau
Auxiliary Bishop
Green Bay, Wisconsin

Notes

1. Dag Hammarskjöld, *Markings,* trans. Leif Sjoberg and W. H. Auden (New York: Alfred A. Knopf, 1981), 93.

2. "Reflections on the Right Use of School Studies with a View to the Love of God," in *The Simone Weil Reader,* ed. George A. Panichas (New York: David MacKay, 1977), 51.

3. Gordon Gilsdorf, *The Same Five Notes* (Francestown, N.H.: Golden Quill Press, 1967), 93.

Acknowledgments

This book is based on a vision that gave rise to the Woodstock Church Leadership Program, inaugurated in 1996 with the financial support of the Raskob Foundation for Catholic Activities. The former director of the Woodstock Theological Center, James L. Connor, S.J., was convinced of the urgent need for the Catholic Church in the United States to respond intelligently, imaginatively, and courageously to the many challenges that rapid change was and is engendering in the culture. He and Msgr. Richard Liddy, a Woodstock fellow (now on the faculty of Seton Hall University), developed a retreat/workshop format to address this need. Select groups of church leaders came together to reflect, in a prayerful atmosphere, on their experiences of leadership in the contemporary Church and to seek a deeper understanding of the kind of leadership Jesus Christ desires for the Church. One clear direction emerged from the seven leadership workshops: namely, the need for commitment to a collaborative model of ministry, both within the Catholic Church (clergy/lay, men/women) and beyond it to collaboration with other churches and community organizations.

During the three years of workshops, a number of Woodstock fellows and associates served as presenters and helped to sharpen the program: Rev. Raymond Kemp, Edmundo Rodriguez, S.J., Thomas J. Reese, S.J., Dr. J. Michael Stebbins, and, of course, James Connor and Richard Liddy. Their pioneering work is evident everywhere in this project.

We saw the book as a necessary next step to allow for a wider church population to benefit from what was learned during those experimental years. The task of transforming lectures and group dynamics into reflective material for individuals and groups, while faithfully conveying the teachings of St. Ignatius and the methodology of Bernard Lonergan, was enormously helped by Michael Stebbins's expertise in these matters. I thank him for his generous gift of time. The interpretation of Lonergan's method, however, is that of the authors. Commentaries on the passages in the Acts of the Apostles (in the Facilitator's Guide) are the contributions of Fr. Edmundo Rodriguez, S.J., who, in turn, is indebted to the insights of Scripture scholar Luke Timothy Johnson.

Brother Dunstan Robidoux, O.S.B., graciously welcomed us to the Lonergan Institute on the grounds of St. Anselm's Abbey in Washington, D.C., so that we could work on the text in the atmosphere of monastic quietude. His own interest in Lonergan, combined with Benedictine hospitality, blessed our work in many ways.

As the text developed, we wanted to see if, indeed, it would be beneficial to a wide variety of leadership groups. Again, with financial support from the Raskob Foundation we were able to field test the materials and fine tune our book. I am deeply grateful to Edmund Gordon, secretary for Christian Formation, Diocese of Wilmington; Helen Lynch Byrnes, pastoral staff, Miraculous Medal Parish, Long Island; Rev. David McDonald, pastor of Blessed Sacrament Parish in Hamden, Connecticut; Robert Moriarty, S.M., coordinator for Small Christian Communities, Archdiocese of Hartford; and Horace Grinnell, pastor of St. Anthony's Parish in Falls Church, Virginia. All of them led leadership groups, met with Woodstock fellows and staff, offered suggestions and directions, and significantly influenced the development of the project. Two other groups, one in New Mexico led by Russell Raskob and another at St. Anselm's Abbey, co-led by the authors (with assistance from Brother Dunstan Robidoux, O.S.B.), provided valuable insights into how effective this particular vision of church leadership can be in a variety of settings.

Words of gratitude are certainly due to the priests, lay leaders, bishops, and religious who participated in the original workshops as Woodstock sought "to get it right." They provided affirmation and critique (both in ample measure) and urged us to continue to share the vision in some way. That's why *Spiritual Exercises for Church Leaders* was produced, and their wisdom is really on every page.

Collaboration, while worthwhile and even necessary, is rarely easy. Collaboration in writing a book can be particularly taxing. In this case, however, working with Paula Minaert has been not only exciting; it has been enlightening. She has the gift of taking complex ideas and making them come alive in story and metaphor. Her love of God and her love for the Church have made this work, and our working together, more beatitude than tribulation.

Finally, invaluable technical assistance, at various stages of the project, was ably and willingly provided by Maria Ferrara, administrative assistant at the Woodstock Center. She lightened our burden considerably.

Dolores R. Leckey
Coordinator
Church Leadership Program
Woodstock Theological Center

Overview

What is the role of the Church in today's world? That role is certainly very different from what it was in the medieval period, when the Catholic Church was the only church and it influenced both the secular and the religious spheres. Now, at the beginning of the third millennium, the Church and the state are firmly separated in most places. Science offers an explanation of the world that sometimes seems to be at odds with the Church's view. We are at a point where technological advances have made possible an affluence that effectively focuses people's attention on the world around them and the things in it — rather than on the Church's mission of bringing about the reign of God, with peace and biblical justice for all. However, the Church's voice, to many people today, appears less confident and less relevant to their lives.

While hardly exhaustive, this is a sampling of the world that the Church lives in now, the world that church leaders — clergy, lay, and religious — must try to understand, with all its diversity. And within this world, leaders face a wide range of difficult issues and problems. No country is immune. In Sudan, Christians are being enslaved, tortured, and killed. In Germany, the Church must respond to violence against immigrants by neo-Nazi groups. In the Netherlands, the Church is fighting recently passed laws that permit assisted suicide, even for children as young as twelve.

In our own country, capital punishment is allowed and abortions are common. In the midst of wealth, many people go without jobs, housing, and food. The popular media projects and promotes an individualistic, consumerist lifestyle. Violence is on the rise. Within the Church, parish leaders worry about the exodus of young people, the so-called Generation Xers, from parish life. They also struggle to respond to the needs of all the people within the parish — families, senior citizens, singles, and various ethnic and racial groups — while at the same time working with the bishop for the mission of the diocesan church. The bishop, in turn, must respond to the needs of all the parishes in the diocese, each of them different.

Also in our country, the Church itself has been racked with severe problems of late. Sexual scandals involving church leaders have arisen in some dioceses, accompanied by accusations of institutional deception. In other places, warring factions within parishes have led to complete dissolution of parish communities. In one town in New York State, a popular pastor began allowing women leaders from the parish to assist him at the liturgies in ways counter to liturgical norms. Some people enthusiastically supported this action, while others strongly opposed it. When the bishop, after many attempts to rectify the situation, had to intervene and transfer the pastor, his supporters left the parish in protest and formed their own community.

How can church leaders carry on the mission of Christ in the midst of all this? How can they help bring Christ's love to a world that seems indifferent, greedy, and self-centered, working within a Church that appears to be more and more fragmented?

First, we must put things into perspective. Our situation is not new. This is not the first time church leaders have lived in a turbulent world or faced seemingly insurmountable internal problems. Over the course of its history, the Church has seen, and survived, the fall of Rome, the Black Death, famine, countless wars, persecution by kings, and much more. It has also faced various heresies, worldly and too-powerful bishops, and warring popes (at one point three different people claimed the title at the same time).

In the early twelfth century, around the towns of Utrecht and Antwerp along the Rhine River, a man named Tanchelm set himself up as a prophet and holy man. He preached against the medieval church and its clergy and gained a huge following among disaffected peasants and workers. They left the Church in droves to follow him, and he lived as a king among them, dispensing his own sacraments and collecting offerings. Tanchelm even declared himself to be God, and his followers believed him, killing anyone who came to take him. No bishop or feudal lord could oppose him. He was finally killed, but even then it took St. Norbert a decade to counter his influence.

Church leaders have always had to deal with problems, both those coming from the outside world and those arising from within. And this is true at the local level as well, because the parish is a microcosm of the wider Church. The issues that parish leaders wrestle with are the same issues facing the whole Church; they're just on a smaller scale.

However — and this is also part of putting things into perspective — we must also understand that these problems and conflicts are not the whole story of the Church. Yes, the Church has always known conflict and upheaval, but it has also known faithfulness to God, and the courage, generosity, and compassion that accompany it. In every age, people have kept their eyes fixed on God and have done God's will. They

have fed the hungry, cared for abandoned children, and rec-
onciled enemies, and have done these things under the aegis
of the Church. The Church has always had to deal with division, corruption, and apathy. But it has also been a way of
nurturing people to great love and self-sacrifice.

The early Middle Ages, after the fall of Rome, is often called
the Dark Ages. This was a time, it seems, when civilization
declined in the West. The art and learning of the ancient world
was forgotten. For most people, every day was a struggle just
to survive. Drought and storms could destroy precious crops;
mysterious diseases often killed both animals and humans.
Feudal lords wielded harsh control over their serfs.

But there was another side to this bleak picture — a light
that came from the Church. The same Church that con-
tained corrupt clergy and warring bishops was also a powerful
force for good. In monasteries and convents across Europe,
people found help and refuge. The monks and nuns welcomed
strangers, cared for the sick, and fed the hungry. In a time
when wars, plagues, and famines were common, their works
of mercy literally meant life for the people. In other ways,
too, they held the world together. It was the monasteries that
preserved the fragments of the ancient world's knowledge in
scrolls and sheets of parchment, carefully copying them and
storing them over the centuries. Their work helped make the
Renaissance possible.

The San Egidio community is a powerful force for good in
today's world. It started in 1968 in Rome, when a young man
sat in the then-rundown church of San Egidio and asked the
Holy Spirit to guide him in his life. Some other young people
joined him in his prayer, and together they waited for God. A

direction became apparent to them; they felt drawn to evangelize and to work with the poor. They began to reach out to children in need, visiting abandoned children living in institutions in Rome and teaching Gypsy children living in camps outside the city. The community found a creative solution to the problem of teaching Gypsy children. Instead of trying to make the children come to conventional classrooms (an approach that had had little success), they went to the Gypsy camps and taught them in abandoned buses there.

The community of San Egidio has grown over the years. It now has about fifteen thousand members, located in Rome and in other cities in Europe, North and South America, and Africa. Members do not formally join; they commit themselves to live the San Egidio vocation: faithful listening to the Gospel in prayer, both personal and liturgical; prompt service to the poor; and support and care for one another.

These people have also committed themselves to peacemaking. They helped organize the Prayer for Peace day in 1986, an interreligious prayer event, and have been involved in peace negotiations in many warring countries. The community has been nominated several times for the Nobel Peace Prize.

Some of us Catholics tend to see the Church as a museum. We walk through it, perhaps regularly but usually not daily. It stays in one place, for the most part, and looks pretty much the same from one year to the next. It's self-contained and it doesn't really change. The problem arises when we notice, as we inevitably do, that it *does* change. The Church is affected by events in the world outside it and by the people inside it — and it always has been. It is a dynamic reality, not static. It is alive.

We often react to this discovery with disorientation and even fear, with the feeling that everything is falling apart. But it isn't falling apart, it's just changing. Change is a vital characteristic of living things. We might do better to see the Church not as a museum but as a living room. We spend a lot of time in it, as we do in a living room. It's where many of the activities of our life happen and where we connect with other people. And it does change over time. We move things around in it as our needs change. We take some items out of the room and bring others into it. It's affected by what we do and by what happens outside it. It is still, however, the living room; its essence doesn't change.

This analogy cannot be stretched too far, obviously. But it does point up the fact that the Church is, and always has been, a living entity rather than a static monolith. What are the implications of this reality for us? We are rooted in Scripture and Tradition. These are the Church's essence, and they give us a firm foundation and a constant form. But within this form, we don't have a fixed set of data that we can memorize and then use to respond to every situation that arises. There is no rule-book, no "Question A requires Answer B." This can make our work as church leaders complicated — but it can also make our work very satisfying. It means we have something akin to a work of art, which, over time, enlightens and enriches our lives, much like a painting or a piece of music.

And our basic question remains the same: how can we as church leaders respond to the needs of our community and the needs of the society in which we live, while remaining faithful to the Church and its teaching?

To find some answers to this question, we turn to the work of a man who lived in the sixteenth century: Iñigo López de Loyola, more commonly known as Ignatius of Loyola. His Spiritual Exercises — a guided retreat exploring the interior life — have been used by Jesuits and, more recently, by other religious and lay people, for more than four hundred years. They are just as rich a guide for personal and spiritual growth now as when they were first written.

But what makes the Exercises useful for church leaders today? They present a profound understanding of human nature and human growth, and then put this understanding into prayer form. Ignatius knew how human beings are constituted and how they behave, and he used this knowledge as a framework for guiding people to an experience of God. The thesis of this book, and of the Church Leadership Program from which it came, is that church leaders need to start with this same fundamental understanding of themselves and other people. This forms the foundation of our spirituality. Then we can begin to understand community — the Church — and we can use this understanding to provide authentic leadership. Leadership thus is an expression of our spirituality.

Why do we start with ourselves? Why use human nature as the basis? Is this any different from secular humanism, which sees the human being, rather than God, as the touchstone for understanding and judging reality? For that matter, how is this approach different from relativism, which holds that, since the individual person is the touchstone, that person's reality *is* reality for him or her? And that therefore there is no objective reality and, consequently, no basis for making moral decisions?

We start with ourselves because we believe that we are made for union with God. This is our blueprint and our call. The more we understand our blueprint, the better we can consciously and willingly respond to our call. Ignatius's Exercises are rooted in this belief. So is the Church Leadership Program.

Another person whose work and insights are central to our program is the Jesuit theologian Bernard Lonergan. In his writings, he addressed the question: How do human beings — whether individual or community — work? Lonergan posited that studying what he called the dynamism of human consciousness was essential to helping church leaders live and serve, and live and serve well, in the modern world.

Goals

Spiritual Exercises for Church Leaders has the following goals:

To help participants . . .

- be attentive in a new way to their experience of themselves as church leaders;

- understand themselves, their communities, the Church, and the world in the context of God's redemptive presence in human history;

- understand the dynamism of human consciousness as essential to authentic church leadership;

- become more adept at discerning the particular ways in which God is calling them and their communities to live lives of discipleship.

One important tool for realizing these goals is the Examen of Saint Ignatius.

The Ignatian Examen

- Become quiet and try to be aware of God's presence. Give God thanks for his great love for you.

- Ask God for the insight to see the Holy Spirit acting in your life and for the grace to understand and respond to the divine call.

- Recall in your mind a specific segment of time — a day, half-day, week, etc. Look for instances of God's presence in your life. What has been happening? How did you respond? Is there a pattern?

- Evaluate what happened in this slice of time and your response to what happened. How did you cooperate with God and God's plan? Give thanks for these occasions. How did you not cooperate? Ask pardon for these occasions.

- Plan how you will collaborate more effectively with God as he acts in your life. Specifically, what do you need to do for this to happen? Prepare to carry it out. Pray for the grace to do it. Close with an Our Father.

Session One

Gratitude

Scripture Passage: Deuteronomy 30:11–14
THE NEARNESS OF GOD

*Surely, this commandment that I am commanding you today
is not too hard for you, nor is it too far away. It is not in heaven,
that you should say, "Who will go up to heaven for us, and
get it for us so that we may hear it and observe it?" Neither is
it beyond the sea, that you should say, "Who will cross to the
other side of the sea for us, and get it for us so that we may
hear it and observe it?" No, the word is very near to you; it is
in your mouth and in your heart for you to observe.*

RUMMAGING FOR GOD:
Praying Backward through Your Day
by Dennis Hamm, S.J.

About twenty years ago, at breakfast and during the few hours
that followed, I had a small revelation. This happened while
I was living in a small community of five Jesuits, all gradu-
ate students in New Haven, Connecticut. I was alone in the
kitchen with my cereal and the *New York Times,* when another
Jesuit came in and said: "I had the weirdest dream just before
I woke up. It was a liturgical dream. The lector had just read
the first reading and proceeded to announce, 'The responsorial refrain today is, *If at first you don't succeed, try, try
again.*' Whereupon the entire congregation soberly repeated,

'If at first you don't succeed, try, try again.' " We both thought this enormously funny. At first, I wasn't sure just *why* this was so humorous. After all, almost everyone would assent to the courageous truth of the maxim, "If at first..." It has to be a cross-cultural truism ("Keep on truckin'"). Why, then, would these words sound so incongruous in a liturgy?

A little later in the day, I stumbled onto a clue. Another, similar phrase popped into my mind: "If today you hear his voice, harden not your hearts" (Ps. 95). It struck me that that sentence has exactly the same rhythm and the same syntax as: "If at first you don't succeed, try, try again." Both begin with an "if" clause and end in an imperative. Both have seven beats. Maybe that was one of the unconscious sources of the humor.

The try-try-again statement sounds like the harden-not-your-heart refrain, yet what a contrast! The latter is clearly biblical, a paraphrase of a verse from a psalm, one frequently used as a responsorial refrain at the Eucharist. The former, you know instinctively, is probably not in the Bible, not even in Proverbs. It is true enough, as far as it goes, but it does not go far enough. There is nothing of faith in it, no sense of God. The sentiment of the line from Psalm 95, however, expresses a conviction central to Hebrew and Christian faith, that we live a life in dialogue with God. The contrast between those two seven-beat lines has, ever since, been for me a paradigm illustrating that truth.

Yet how do we hear the voice of God? Our Christian tradition has at least four answers to that question. First, along with the faithful of most religions, we perceive the divine in what God has made, creation itself (that insight sits at the heart of Christian moral thinking). Second, we hear God's voice in the Scriptures, which we even call "the word of God." Third, we hear God in the authoritative teaching of the Church, the living tradition of our believing community. Finally, we hear God by attending to our experience and interpreting it in the light of all those other ways of hearing the divine voice — the structures of creation, the Bible, the living tradition of the community.

The phrase, "If *today* you hear his voice," implies that the divine voice must somehow be accessible in our daily experience, for we are creatures who live one day at a time. If God wants to communicate with us, it has to happen in the course of a twenty-four-hour day, for we live in no other time. And how do we go about this kind of listening? Long tradition has provided a helpful tool, which we call the examination of consciousness today. "Rummaging for God" is an expression that suggests going through a drawer full of stuff, feeling around, looking for something that you are sure must be in there somewhere. I think that image catches some of the feel of what is classically known in church language as the prayer of "Examen."

The Examen, or examination, of conscience is an ancient practice in the Church. In fact, even before Christianity, the Pythagoreans and the Stoics promoted a version of the practice. It is what most of us Catholics were taught to do to prepare for confession. In that form, the Examen was a matter of examining one's life in terms of the Ten Commandments to see how daily behavior stacked up against those divine criteria. St. Ignatius includes it as one of the exercises in his manual *The Spiritual Exercises.*

It is still a salutary thing to do but wears thin as a lifelong, daily practice. It is hard to motivate yourself to keep searching your experience for how you sinned. In recent decades, spiritual writers have worked with the implication that *conscience* in Romance languages like French (*conscience*) and Spanish (*conciencia*) means more than our English word "conscience," in the sense of moral awareness and judgment; it also means "consciousness."

Now prayer that deals with the full contents of your *consciousness* lets you cast your net much more broadly than prayer that limits itself to the contents of conscience, or moral awareness. A number of people — most famously, George Aschenbrenner, S.J., in an article in *Review for Religious* (1971) — have developed this idea in profoundly practical ways. Recently, the Institute of Jesuit Sources in St. Louis published a fascinating reflection by Joseph Tetlow, S.J., called *The Most Postmodern Prayer: American Jesuit Identity and the Examen of Conscience, 1920–1990.*

What I am proposing here is a way of doing the Examen that works for me. It puts a special emphasis on feelings, for reasons that I hope will become apparent. First, I describe the format. Second, I invite you to spend a few minutes actually doing it. Third, I describe some of the consequences that I have discovered to flow from this kind of prayer.

A Five-Step Method

1. *Pray for light.* Since we are not simply daydreaming or reminiscing but rather looking for some sense of how the Spirit of God is leading us, it only makes sense to pray for some illumination. The goal is not simply memory, but graced understanding. That's a gift from God devoutly to be begged. "Lord, help me understand this blooming, buzzing confusion."

2. *Review the day in thanksgiving.* Note how different this is from looking immediately for your sins. Nobody likes to poke around in the memory bank to uncover smallness, weakness, lack of generosity. But everybody likes to fondle beautiful gifts, and that is precisely what the past twenty-four hours contain — gifts of existence,

work, relationships, food, challenges. Gratitude is the foundation of our whole relationship with God. So use whatever cues help you to walk through the day from the moment of awakening — even the dreams you recall upon awakening. Walk through the past twenty-four hours, from hour to hour, from place to place, task to task, person to person, thanking the Lord for every gift you encounter.

3. *Review the feelings that surface in the play of the day.* Our feelings, positive and negative, the painful and the pleasing, are clear signals of where the action was during the day. Simply pay attention to any and all of those feelings as they surface, the whole range: delight, boredom, fear, anticipation, resentment, anger, peace, contentment, impatience, desire, hope, regret, shame, uncertainty, compassion, disgust, gratitude, pride, rage, doubt, confidence, admiration, shyness — whatever was there. Some of us may be hesitant to focus on feelings in this over-psychologized age, but I believe that these feelings are the liveliest index to what is happening in our lives. This leads us to the fourth moment.

4. *Choose one of those feelings (positive or negative) and pray from it.* That is, choose the remembered feeling that most caught your attention. The feeling is a sign that something important was going on. Now simply express spontaneously the prayer that surfaces as you attend to the source of the feeling — praise, petition, contrition, cry for help or healing, whatever.

5. *Look toward tomorrow.* Using your appointment calendar if that helps, face your immediate future. What

feelings surface as you look at the tasks, meetings, and appointments that face you? Fear? Delighted anticipation? Self-doubt? Temptation to procrastinate? Zestful planning? Regret? Weakness? Whatever it is, turn it into prayer — for help, for healing, whatever comes spontaneously. To round off the Examen, say the Lord's Prayer.

A mnemonic for recalling the five points: LT3Fs (light, thanks, feelings, focus, future). Try it! Take a few minutes to pray through the past twenty-four hours, and toward the next twenty-four hours, with that five-point format.

Consequences

Here are some consequences flowing from this kind of prayer:

1. There is always something to pray about. For a person who does this kind of prayer at least once a day, there is never the question: What should I talk to God about? Until you die, you always have a past twenty-four hours, and you always have some feelings about what's next.

2. The gratitude moment is worthwhile in itself. "Dedicate yourselves to gratitude," Paul tells the Colossians. Even if we drift off into slumber after reviewing the gifts of the day, we have praised the Lord.

3. We learn to face the Lord where we are, as we are. There is no other way to be present to God, of course, but we often fool ourselves into thinking that we have to "put on our best face" before we address our God.

4. We learn to respect our feelings. Feelings count. They are morally neutral until we make some choice about

acting upon or dealing with them. But if we don't attend to them, we miss what they have to tell us about the quality of our lives.

5. Praying from feelings, we are liberated from them. An unattended emotion can dominate and manipulate us. Attending to and praying from and about the persons and situations that give rise to the emotions helps us to cease being unwitting slaves of our emotions.

6. We actually find something to bring to confession. That is, we stumble across our sins without making them the primary focus.

7. We can experience an inner healing. People have found that praying about (as opposed to fretting about or denying) feelings leads to a healing of mental life. We probably get a head start on our dreamwork when we do this.

8. This kind of prayer helps us get over our Deism. Deism is belief in a sort of "clockmaker" God, a God who does indeed exist but does not have much, if anything, to do with his people's ongoing life. The God we have come to know through our Jewish and Christian experience is more present than we usually think.

9. Praying this way is an antidote to the spiritual disease of Pelagianism. Pelagianism was the heresy that approached life with God as a do-it-yourself project ("If at first you don't succeed..."), whereas a true theology of grace and freedom sees life as response to God's love ("If today you hear God's voice...").

A final thought. How can anyone dare to say that paying attention to felt experience is a listening to the voice of God?

On the face of it, it does sound like a dangerous presumption. But, notice, I am not equating memory with the voice of God. I am saying that, if we are to listen for the God who creates and sustains us, we need to take seriously and prayerfully the meeting between the creatures we are and all else that God holds lovingly in existence. That "interface" is the felt experience of my day. It deserves prayerful attention. It is a big part of how we know and respond to God.

Work Pages for Session One (pages 33–35)

Scripture Notes: Deuteronomy 30:11–14
THE NEARNESS OF GOD

Exercise: Gratitude

I am grateful for . . .

Session Notes

Preparation for Session Two

1. Ignatius said that every sin, at its heart, is a sin of ingratitude. Reflect on this statement. What do you think he meant by this? Do you agree with it? Why or why not?

2. Read Acts of the Apostles, chapter 10, verses 1–23. The group will be discussing this passage at the beginning of the next session.

3. Try to do the Examen at home over the next week. The group will do it together in Session Three. For background on it, read the article by Dennis Hamm beginning on page 25 of this book. Take notes on your experience.

4. Read ahead the sections in Session Two titled "Sin" and "Being Attentive" (pages 38–44).

Session Two

Being Attentive

Scripture Passage: Acts 10:1–23
PETER'S VISION

In Caesarea there was a man named Cornelius, a centurion of the Italian Cohort, as it was called. He was a devout man who feared God with all his household; he gave alms generously to the people and prayed constantly to God. One afternoon at about three o'clock he had a vision in which he clearly saw an angel of God coming in and saying to him, "Cornelius." He stared at him in terror and said, "What is it, Lord?" He answered, "Your prayers and your alms have ascended as a memorial before God. Now send men to Joppa for a certain Simon who is called Peter; he is lodging with Simon, a tanner, whose house is by the seaside." When the angel who spoke to him had left, he called two of his slaves and a devout soldier from the ranks of those who served him, and after telling them everything, he sent them to Joppa.

About noon the next day, as they were on their journey and approaching the city, Peter went up on the roof to pray. He became hungry and wanted something to eat; and while it was being prepared, he fell into a trance. He saw the heaven opened and something like a large sheet coming down, being lowered to the ground by its four corners. In it were all kinds of four-footed creatures and reptiles and birds of the air. Then he heard a voice saying, "Get up, Peter; kill and eat." But Peter said, "By no means, Lord; for I have never eaten anything that

37

is profane or unclean." The voice said to him again, a second time, "What God has made clean, you must not call profane." This happened three times, and the thing was suddenly taken up to heaven.

Now while Peter was greatly puzzled about what to make of the vision that he had seen, suddenly the men sent by Cornelius appeared. They were asking for Simon's house and were standing by the gate. They called out to ask whether Simon, who was called Peter, was staying there. While Peter was still thinking about the vision, the Spirit said to him, "Look, three men are searching for you. Now get up, go down, and go with them without hesitation; for I have sent them." So Peter went down to the men and said, "I am the one you are looking for; what is the reason for your coming?" They answered, "Cornelius, a centurion, an upright and God-fearing man, who is well spoken of by the whole Jewish nation, was directed by a holy angel to send for you to come to his house and to hear what you have to say." So Peter invited them in and gave them lodging.

Sin

If you remember from the Examen, the second step is asking God for the grace to be aware of sin in our life. The whole first week of Ignatius's Spiritual Exercises focuses on becoming aware of sin — how sin is inextricably part of our lives and part of the wider world around us.

Many people today are uncomfortable with this approach. They believe that looking at sin is negative and counter-productive, a return to earlier times when religion seemed to consist primarily of lamenting our sins and fearing God's judgment.

This was not Ignatius's intention, however. Remember that the Exercises take place within the context of gratitude. We begin by giving thanks to God, the creator of the universe and the giver of all gifts. We acknowledge that we come from God and are moving toward God. Our purpose is rooted in God. So we start by looking at God and his creation and his plan — not at ourselves.

Only then do we look at the places where this creation is disrupted, this plan broken, due to human actions. This is how Ignatius viewed sin: a deliberate rejection of God's order. Joseph Tetlow, S.J., in his book about the Exercises, says that today we are more likely to experience sin as a damaging or a breaking of our relationship with God, with others, and with ourselves.

But sin is more than an individual person breaking rules or breaking relationships, although this is certainly part of it. Sin also has a social aspect, what we call social sin. We can describe social sin as the expression and effect of personal sins. But it is more than an exercise in mathematics. We don't just add individuals' personal sins and end up with a social sin. Nor can we simply subtract individuals' personal sins from a social sin and thus lessen it. Social sin is woven into the very fabric of human communities. The structure of society often works systematically to harm certain people within it. Those victims, of course, are caught in this sinful structure, but so are other people: those who benefit from the system, even unknowingly; those who administer the system, who may not even approve of it but cannot change it; and finally those who use the system to their own advantage. Individual guilt varies, but all are part of the sinful situation that is allowed to exist.

Social sin often results from our inheriting distorted views of reality. If our parents and grandparents, and everyone we know, and every book and newspaper we read, all assume that certain people are inferior, we will probably adopt this view as well. We will also probably copy the behavior that goes along with it. So mistaken and distorted views and sinful behavior spread throughout a community and are passed along in time.

The slavery that existed in our country into the nineteenth century is a good example of a social sin. It may seem that only the people who actually owned or sold slaves were guilty of sin, but the sin affected our whole country. Factories in the North made, and profited from the sale of, cloth from the cotton picked by slaves. Northerners who never owned slaves bought and used the cloth. Slavery touched everyone in one way or another.

Social sins still exist today. The U.S. bishops, in their statement *In All Things Charity* (issued 1999), name some of them: the drug trade, the recycling of illicit funds, corruption at every level, the terror of violence, the arms race, racial discrimination, inequality between social groups, and the irrational destruction of nature. You will notice that these sins are far-reaching and complicated. They affect all of us, just as slavery did. Whole communities can be corrupted and distorted by sin.

Sin, then, is a pervasive part of our lives and the world around us. It is a sharp reminder of how much we human beings fall short of the glory of God. Yet this awareness of sin does not mean we should despair or give up. It is, rather, the first step toward repenting. Another way of understanding repentance is to see it as our attempt to mend the ruptures in our lives, to repair our relationship with God and with others. Only by doing this can we take our rightful place in God's world and truly follow God and do his will. And only then can we move closer to God.

Being Attentive

How does this growth happen? It requires conscious change on our part. Real growth never occurs without change. And this change and this growth need to happen not just within individuals but within the community, the Church, as well. This growth toward God is our goal. Facilitating it is our task as church leaders.

The first step in changing is to become aware of the breaks, to recognize the damage. This is also the second step of the Examen, where Ignatius instructs us to ask God for the grace to know sin in our life. From our perspective, since we know that these ruptures, these breaks in God's creation, are found everywhere, we are being asked to look at the whole of our life and the world around us. We are not following God as we should; we are broken. The world is not doing God's will either; it too is broken. This is what Ignatius labeled sin.

What's more, God is actively involved in the world and our lives. God is a God of history. Therefore, everything about us and everything that happens, all our experiences, are places to look for God. This, perhaps, is why some people have said that sin is an opportunity. When we pay attention to what goes on inside ourselves and in the world, we cannot help but see the presence and work of God. We begin to see God's call and how we have responded to it — or not responded to it. The more we are attentive, the better we can begin to discern this call and the more we learn about how to conform ourselves to God.

Bernard Lonergan labeled this deliberate observation as the first imperative: Be attentive! It is the first stage in the process of how we humans truly respond to God.

Let's examine why observation is so important, why we need to be attentive. The answer lies in our basic makeup as human beings. Look at babies. They enter the world with a blank slate. Everything is new to them; nothing is familiar. They take in information through the experiences of their senses, but this information has no meaning for them. Nothing even has a name, since babies have no language with which to identify things. Everything is immediate.

Our main task as human beings is to make sense of our world. As infants, we are totally open to everything that happens to us. Our experiences affect us directly. Almost everything that happens in our world is important to us because there are few barriers between our selves and what we perceive. As we grow, we learn to distinguish, separate, categorize, and label. As we acquire language, we learn the names of things, and this too helps us make meaning. But it also means that we erect barriers. We put some things at a distance from us, or we become unable to see certain things because we have learned that they have no meaning for us.

We do not accomplish this task in isolation. In fact, we couldn't do it by ourselves. Our parents and the other people in our environment play a vital role in this process. They teach us about the world around us, both directly (by what they tell us) and indirectly (by how they interact with us). The way we make sense of our world comes through others and is profoundly affected by them. To a certain extent, these other people are handing on their meaning to us.

It is not only the people right around us who shape the world we construct for ourselves. Our whole culture does, starting from when we are infants and continuing throughout our lives. It is largely a hidden influence, something we rarely notice. To give an example, we North Americans are a nation of meat eaters. We also live mostly in cities and suburbs. Very few of us are farmers. We don't often see live cows. Our main contact with cows is probably as decorations for our kitchens, on towels, potholders, and cream pitchers. We simply don't think about them very much.

On the other hand, Hindus, from time immemorial, have held cows in high esteem for all these animals give to us: milk, butter, cream, cheese. They would never think of slaughtering them. Consequently, cows are everywhere in India. They wander freely, grazing where they wish. In the cities, cars yield the right-of-way to them. It's the same animal as the one in our country, but it's not.

Closer to home, think about the way different people might see a statue of the Virgin Mary. Catholics may see someone important in their lives, a comforting figure familiar to them from childhood. Some Protestants may see a source of division between themselves and Catholics. It's the same statue, but it's not.

We construct our world according to what's important to us, based on what we have learned from our experiences. But, obviously, our world has boundaries, limits. For all of us, there are things we don't know, things we don't care about, and things we can't even ask questions about. We also, as was mentioned earlier, have mistakes in our world — incomplete understandings, distorted perceptions, inaccurate ideas. Some we did not even choose; we inherited them. Others arise from our own experiences or decisions. But we need to realize that these mistakes do exist, that our horizons are imperfect.

It is essential to be attentive to our horizons. We need to step back and observe the world we've constructed, try to see it objectively. Why? Horizons — those of individuals and those of communities — can change. Sometimes these changes are minor; sometimes they are sudden and far-reaching. Conversion — a radical shift in consciousness that puts us in a different place — is a major change in horizons. We see the world in a new way.

Conversion is necessary in order to be authentic leaders. Many people drift into their horizons. Outside forces have pushed them into their world, and they have not really been aware of the process. They know only their own world and cannot see past their horizons. They accept their world as all there is; they become complacent.

Leaders are the people who take responsibility for their world as they have constructed it. They realize that it's up to them to decide what they will make of themselves. They ask themselves the questions: Is this way that I see the world, the way I've made my world, accurate? Is it helpful?

Work Pages for Session Two (pages 45–48)

Scripture Notes: Acts 10:1–23
PETER'S VISION

Example: Horizons of a Laywoman

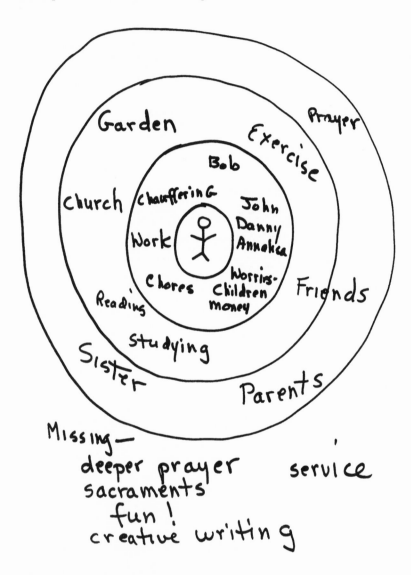

This example is to be used in conjunction with the Facilitator's presentation on horizons.

Exercise: My Horizons
(To be done in the group)

Session Notes

Preparation for Session Three

1. Read in the Acts of the Apostles chapter 10, verses 23 to 35. Pay attention to the two uses of words having to do with sight.

2. Choose one day during the next week and try to be attentive to your experience throughout that day. What happens around you, with the people in your community? What happens within you? How do you react to what happens? Where do your time and energy go? What was consoling? What was problematic? Are you pleased with what you notice? Do you see any patterns? What are they? Write down your thoughts.

3. Read the articles in this book on exploring (being intelligent) on pages 51–55: "A Lesson in Semantics," "The Dynamism of Consciousness," and "A Personal Narrative."

Session Three

Exploring (Being Intelligent)

Scripture Passage: Acts 10:23–35
PETER AND CORNELIUS

The next day he got up and went with them, and some of the believers from Joppa accompanied him. The following day they came to Caesarea. Cornelius was expecting them and had called together his relatives and close friends. On Peter's arrival Cornelius met him, and falling at his feet, worshiped him. But Peter made him get up, saying, "Stand up; I am only a mortal." And as he talked with him, he went in and found that many had assembled; and he said to them, "You yourselves know that it is unlawful for a Jew to associate with or to visit a Gentile; but God has shown me that I should not call anyone profane or unclean. So when I was sent for, I came without objection. Now may I ask why you sent for me?"

Cornelius replied, "Four days ago at this very hour, at three o'clock, I was praying in my house when suddenly a man in dazzling clothes stood before me. He said, 'Cornelius, your prayer has been heard and your alms have been remembered before God. Send therefore to Joppa and ask for Simon, who is called Peter; he is staying in the home of Simon, a tanner, by the sea.' Therefore I sent for you immediately, and you have been kind enough to come. So now all of us are here in the presence of God to listen to all that the Lord has commanded you to say."

Then Peter began to speak to them: "I truly understand that God shows no partiality, but in every nation anyone who fears him and does what is right is acceptable to him."

A Lesson in Semantics

"Exploring," as the word is used in this context, does not mean a willingness to jump up out of our seats and go to a distant land, like the Jumblies in Edward Lear's poem. It's not a physical or geographical endeavor (at least, not usually). It involves, rather, a state of mind; it is more an interior thing. But it is similar to that first understanding, because it describes a willingness to ask questions about the world and everything in it: ourselves, our ideas, other people, our culture. It means we do not take things for granted because we know that our understanding is imperfect and incomplete. There is always more to be learned, more to discover, about everything. It refers both to the effort of trying to understand things and make sense of things, and the process of actually understanding them.

Bernard Lonergan spoke of exploring, too, only he called it being intelligent. By this, he meant not improving one's intellectual abilities but the same active questioning, exploring, and having insights as described above. In his thinking, it is the second imperative (the first was being attentive), the second part of the process of how our consciousness is structured and how it operates.

Ignatius, too, stresses the importance of exploring. We see this connection in the third step in his Examen, which he calls the Review. In this step, you recall in your mind a specific segment of time in your life — for example, a day, a half-day. You look for instances of God at work during this time, and you ask questions about it. What is happening? What is going on under the surface? This is not mere observation but an active effort to understand.

When we do this, we are trying to understand our world, the world we have constructed for ourselves. As you recall, each person constructs his or her own world, starting at birth. This is how we make sense of our environment, and it's how we learn and grow. We need to do this. But, having said this, we also need to realize that our world doesn't correspond exactly with *the* world. As we have already learned, we all have boundaries — what we've called our horizons, which is the sum total of what we look at and how we look at it. Our horizons form the limits of our world.

In trying to understand our world, we step back a bit. We look at what we have considered to be reality and realize that it is shaped (or even distorted) by our horizons. The very act of questioning something, in our environment or in ourselves, causes us to consider the possibility that it may not be what we thought it was. This can be very disorienting — and we often resist doing it — but it is crucial. As we ask questions, as we gather facts, we are better able to see God acting in our life and how we are responding to this action. We are able to ask ourselves if our horizons have prevented us from seeing what God is asking of us, or if God is gently pushing us to expand our horizons.

This work of trying to understand our own world helps us to be more aware of other people's worlds. It reinforces for us the realization that everyone has constructed a world for himself or herself, and each is different. This is significant, because it means that no two people see things in exactly the same way. No two people assign meaning to reality in exactly the same way. It's not just that people view reality differently, but that the realities within which they live *are* different.

As was explained earlier, people's worlds can — and do — overlap some of the time. To the extent that our world overlaps with someone else's, we can talk and cooperate with that person. We can speak of *our* world. But people's worlds can also be very far apart from each other, with nothing at all in common. And sometimes they can collide.

This is why we ask questions. We come to understand ourselves and our world, and we can start trying to bring our world closer to *the* world — God's world. And the more we accept the ongoing need to hold our world up to questioning and discernment (Lonergan's whole dynamism of consciousness), the more we are able to understand and work with other people. It is essential for leaders.

The Dynamism of Consciousness

The dynamism of consciousness has four capacities, four elements. We are constantly moving through these capacities, in a spiral of sorts. Within each capacity, as we work with it, we sense questions. It is these questions that move us on to the next capacity.

The first capacity is **being attentive.** We have already talked about this, in Session Two. This happens at the level of experience — when we use our senses, when we imagine things, when we notice things. It's when we pay attention to what is going on around us and within us. It means, as we did in the exercise last week, trying to step back and notice our noticing. Then, the questions we feel are: What's going on? What's the explanation? These questions take us to the second capacity.

The second capacity is **exploring, being intelligent, trying to understand.** We gather data. We look for clues, ideas, connections; we form hypotheses. We are trying to make sense of what we're experiencing, trying to find a pattern that explains it and gives it meaning. Then the question we ask is: Is my explanation correct? This takes us to the third capacity.

The third capacity is **discerning.** This is the level of judgment. We're trying to discern what is real and true, based on the questions we've asked and the evidence we've collected. We are testing our understanding. Once we have done this, we ask: What should I do? This leads us to the fourth capacity.

The fourth capacity is **being responsible.** This is the level of decision. Now that we have gathered facts, come to an understanding of them, and made a judgment about them — we act. We take a stand; we make choices. We use what we have learned from the three previous steps to decide what is real, what is true, what is valuable, and we base our action on this judgment.

A Personal Narrative:
An Example of Personal Authenticity

John Henry Newman lived in England in the nineteenth century (1801–1890), but his life and his experience — especially his spiritual quest — speak powerfully to people today. He first became known as an educator, pastor, and spokesman for the Church of England, and then caused a great controversy by converting to the Roman Catholic Church. He was made a cardinal and was one of the Church's foremost writers and thinkers. Today, he is sometimes called one of the fathers of the Second Vatican Council, for his influence on it.

The young Newman studied at Oxford, won a teaching fellowship at one of the colleges there, and was ordained in the Church of England. He expected a life devoted to education and the care of souls. This is, in fact, what he received, but not in the way he had imagined.

Newman began moving toward what was called a middle way, one that believed that the Church of England was not a form of Protestantism but part of the Catholic Church — though it was anti-Roman. This brought him into conflict with the Oxford authorities, a conflict that only increased when Newman became part of the Oxford Movement. The movement called for the spiritual renewal of the Church of England by returning to its Catholic roots.

For fifteen years Newman struggled for the renewal of the Church — and he struggled with himself. Gradually he realized that positions he had previously held were no longer tenable and that commitment to Christ demanded that he undertake new public commitments. Finally, in 1845, after long years of prayer and discernment, he left the Anglican Church and "all he held dear" to become a Roman Catholic. He was following his conscience, his inner light, though doing so proved heartwrenching. As he had once written in an essay: "In another world it might be different, but here below to live is to change and to be perfect is to have changed often."

Newman entered the Church of Rome, having decided that its teachings were truly Catholic and that it was the "one, holy, catholic, and apostolic church." His decision — his entire journey — was a commitment to both reason, the life of the mind, and experience. It is interesting that, after all his intellectual efforts, he described his awareness at joining the Catholic Church as less of a change than a "coming into port after a rough sea."

Work Pages for Session Three (pages 56–58)

Scripture Notes: Acts 10:23–35
PETER AND CORNELIUS

Exercise: Doing the Examen

Session Notes

Preparation for Session Four

1. Read in the Acts of the Apostles chapter 10, verses 36 to 48, and reflect on the passage.

2. Write a personal narrative of your own. Describe an experience in your role as a church leader in which you changed your mind about something. It could be something external or something internal. Then analyze the experience. What happened? What was your understanding before the experience? How did your new understanding come to you? How did you feel? Be specific. (You can use the space on page 60.)

3. Read the articles on pages 63–68.

4. Take time to reflect on the meditation on the Trinity, the Annunciation, and the Incarnation (beginning on page 70 of this book). The drawings are part of it. You may write your impressions down on page 61.

Assignment: Personal Narrative

To be completed between Sessions Three and Four.

Assignment: Meditation on the Trinity, the Annunciation, and the Incarnation

After you have read and reflected on the meditation beginning on page 70 (text and pictures), write your response here.

Session Four

Discerning

Scripture Passage: Acts 10:36–48
PETER AND A ROMAN

You know the message he sent to the people of Israel, preach-
ing peace by Jesus Christ — he is Lord of all. That message
spread throughout Judea, beginning in Galilee after the bap-
tism that John announced: how God anointed Jesus of Naza-
reth with the Holy Spirit and with power; how he went about
doing good and healing all who were oppressed by the devil,
for God was with him. We are witnesses to all that he did both
in Judea and in Jerusalem. They put him to death by hang-
ing him on a tree; but God raised him on the third day and
allowed him to appear, not to all the people but to us who
were chosen by God as witnesses, and who ate and drank
with him after he rose from the dead. He commanded us to
preach to the people and to testify that he is the one ordained
by God as judge of the living and the dead. All the prophets
testify about him that everyone who believes in him receives
forgiveness of sins through his name.

While Peter was still speaking, the Holy Spirit fell upon
all who heard the word. The circumcised believers who had
come with Peter were astounded that the gift of the Holy Spirit
had been poured out even on the Gentiles, for they heard them
speaking in tongues and extolling God. Then Peter said, "Can
anyone withhold the water for baptizing these people who
have received the Holy Spirit just as we have?" So he ordered

them to be baptized in the name of Jesus Christ. Then they invited him to stay for several days.

We Do Not Live in a Vacuum

We have all heard the expression, "Nature abhors a vacuum." In science, this means that when a vacuum does exist — a space without air, without oxygen, nitrogen, or any matter at all — those elements that lie outside of it try to move into it to fill it. In the televised pictures of astronauts walking on the moon or floating in space near their spaceship, they wear spacesuits and breathing masks because they are in a vacuum. Watching them, we are well aware that if those masks are punctured the astronauts are doomed, because the life-giving air they contain then rushes out to try to fill the huge emptiness surrounding them.

Physically, biologically, we human beings cannot live in a vacuum. We know this. We live within an atmosphere that provides all the elements we need in order to survive. This is also true, however, on a metaphorical level. We are all born into families, cultures, religions, tribes, and nations. We need this atmosphere if we are to survive and grow, if we are to be truly human. If we do not have it, we lack something vital. We know this from observing the phenomenon of feral children, those children who grow up literally without any human contact at all because of either abandonment or abuse. These children can sometimes learn enough to make up for their deprivations, if they are found at a young enough age. But the point is that we human beings are meant to live in an environment with other human beings and with all the things that they create: families, cultures, and so on.

Interestingly enough, since this environment is so crucial, we are not even very aware of it a good deal of the time. It surrounds us like an atmosphere and, like an atmosphere, we pay little attention to it. We talked about this earlier, when we discussed the fact that we human beings construct our own worlds, which are heavily influenced by the environment in which we live.

How is this environment connected with discerning, which is the third of the human capacities that Bernard Lonergan describes? How is it connected with the dynamism of consciousness, the fundamental way in which we operate? To begin with, this dynamism happens, in each of us, within a certain context, within our own unique world. And this world affects the dynamism as it unfolds. It influences what we pay attention to, the kinds of questions we can ask, the judgments we make, and the actions we take.

This is especially relevant to discerning, the capacity of making judgments. We do not make judgments in isolation, but within the world we have constructed. Different people can have the same experience, can be attentive to the same details, can ask the same or similar questions, but still form very different judgments. For example, a person committed to the Church and to the spiritual life will go through the same process as a person who is a member of the criminal underworld. All human beings work the same way. But how these two individuals discern a situation, and what they do about it, will vary tremendously, because their worlds — from which they derive their values — are so different.

What's more, even people who would appear to inhabit the same world can reach very different conclusions. We know that Christians can — and do — disagree violently about a number of things. In the early church, as we read in Acts, members had very divergent opinions about who was eligible for baptism and what the criteria were for being accepted as a follower of Jesus.

In discerning, this third capacity, we have already paid attention to a situation and we have collected information about it. We have asked questions. We have had an insight or reached an explanation. Now we need to make a judgment. In order to do this, we need to put this explanation into a context, a framework. But what context should we use? We have seen the limitations of the world that we construct for ourselves. We know that our world does not equal *the* world.

Discerning means we try to make our own world closer to, more reflective of, God's world. When we do this, we are entering — and encountering — truth. We are facing up to things as they are, and this includes our own effect on things, which is never easy to perceive.

Ignatius's Examen also touches on discerning in the third step, which he called asking pardon. When we enter the real world, the truth, we are able to see the occasions and places where God's will has been rejected, either by us or by others. We see where his plan for the world has been disrupted. We see where our relationship with God and with others has been broken. In other words, we discern sin for what it is and we are able to recognize and accept it as such. And we ask pardon for our complicity in it.

A Study in Discernment: Using Progress/Decline/Redemption

A powerful tool for discernment — one developed by Bernard Lonergan — is what he called progress/decline/redemption. These are the three fundamental movements in human history. Using this lens provides us with a way of understanding both what has gone on in the past and what is happening now, and it helps us as we move toward the future. This lens applies to our personal lives and to our life in community.

Progress occurs when we are authentic, when we are true to our best selves. We know we are authentic when we are trying to be faithful to our internal dynamism, to using the four capacities that Lonergan describes. This process happens both in our personal lives and within our communities; the struggle for authenticity takes place on both levels. We can see it all through human history.

When we are inauthentic, we have decline. This means that we are ignoring or rejecting our internal dynamism; we are refusing to respond to the call for growth, the call that is built into our very selves. Decline, too, happens in communities and has always been part of our history.

Finally, we have redemption. Redemption is God acting in the world, offering us grace, giving us another chance to cooperate with him. We do not bring this about; it is God's gift. Our role is to respond to this grace. When we do, amazing things happen. We human beings can be and do more than we had ever imagined.

This may seem very abstract. What might progress/decline/redemption look like in real life? How can we apply it? To find out, let's take an example with which we are probably quite familiar: Western Europe, particularly Germany, before and during the Second World War.

Many historians believe that the seeds of the Second World War, in Europe at least, were sown in the First World War. Germany's economy was struggling, many of its towns were in ruins, and its people had suffered terrible losses. While this was true for most of Europe, Germany also had, as conditions of the treaty that ended the war, very harsh political and financial sanctions imposed on it by its enemies. The Allied powers wanted to ensure that Germany would never again be a threat to its neighbors. All this led to feelings of great bitterness among the German people, historians say, feelings that (combined with the grim economic situation) led directly to the rise of Hitler and the Second World War. That second conflict was inevitable.

But history is rarely this simple. There was not necessarily a straight downward line that went from the first to the second war. There is, in some people's opinions, at least the possibility that Germany could have chosen another course of action. As evidence, they point to the decades of the 1920s and the 1930s, when a profound and influential artistic life flourished in Germany. What makes this significant is that the arts community comprised Jewish as well as non-Jewish members. Artists, musicians, and singers all worked together in the service of art, with little divisiveness because of religion. And the people in the country, in turn, welcomed these artists with a similar lack of concern for such distinctions. One group of musicians, called the Comedian Harmonists, was wildly popular. Made up of three Jewish and two non-Jewish members, they performed a unique blend of operetta, American-style jazz, and children's nonsense songs. Sadly, the group was forced to disband when Hitler came to power. But some modern historians believe that this group, along with the rest of the arts community in Germany, was evidence of something good going on at a time when it appeared that things were all negative. This is progress. Some people were paying attention to their internal dynamism and were being true to their best selves. It did not prevent the war or the Holocaust from occurring, but it was a positive element that did influence people's lives for the better, if only temporarily.

Decline, in our example, is all too familiar. We all know the story of how Hitler took over Germany, attacked neighboring countries, and ordered the murder of millions of Jews, Gypsies, and other "undesirables." Millions of other people were brutalized, whether they were among the conquered or the victors. "Ordinary" Germans went along with Hitler's cruelty and destruction, either directly by participating in it or indirectly by condoning it or not resisting it. They seemed to be controlled by the worst in themselves, which is one way of describing decline.

Yet even in the midst of the horror, we can see redemption. Recent research has shown that there were many ordinary Germans who sheltered and otherwise helped Jews who were hiding. They hid them in their homes, fed and clothed them, obtained false identity papers and, when it was too dangerous for them to stay, sent them on to another person who would hide them. These men and women not only received nothing for their efforts, they were risking their own lives. Some of them were caught and punished, a powerful reminder of the self-sacrificing nature of redemption. What's more, the numbers of these people are not small. One contemporary historian has estimated that for every Jewish person who managed to hide from the government, some twenty to fifty non-Jewish people were involved. Some of these people are still alive today and have been recognized and honored for what they did. In interviews, most of them simply say, "It was the right thing to do." They were following the best in themselves and responding to God's grace. Today, these people are recognized and honored in Israel's Garden of the Righteous at Yad Vashem.

Work Pages for Session Four (pages 69–76)

Scripture Notes: Acts 10:36–48
PETER AND A ROMAN

Exercise: Meditation on the Trinity, the Annunciation, and the Incarnation

Note: The following meditation is based on a meditation in Ignatius's Spiritual Exercises. If you want to look at the original meditation, see Joseph Tetlow's book, *Ignatius Loyola: Spiritual Exercises.* The heart of the meditation is reflecting on the decision made by the Trinity for God to join humanity. The pictures here are meant to stimulate your thinking and your prayer. The first three pictures depict what the Trinity saw looking across time and space, what led the Trinity to the Incarnation. The fourth picture is of Mary, who is part of that decision.

We start by seeing a secret place,
a place that is nowhere
we have ever been.
It is not on this earth;
it was before the earth was made.
It is this moment and every moment.
It was before time began
and before the universe existed.
It is now and forever.

From this place where matter is not
and this time where time is not,
the Trinity looks at the earth.
The Trinity looks at the people of the earth.
The Trinity sees all the men and women
who have ever lived
since the world was made.

stephen a. titra

stephen a. titra

stephen a. titra

In this place sits the Trinity:
God the Father, God the Son,
God the Holy Spirit.
God creates.
God saves.
God sanctifies.
All this because God loves.
The Trinity is one in love.
The Trinity *is* love.

ANNUNCIATION

Were others asked?

A lassie from an isle in a distant sea?
A maiden in North Africa
or a slave girl from the Congo?
How many times were angels sent
and returned, unheard, unheeded?
Was Mary tenth on salvation's list,
or the hundredth?

And you, my soul,
was "fiat" spoken
when the angel came?

—Robert F. Morneau

Session Notes

Preparation for Session Five

1. Read Acts 11:1–18. Reflect on the passage.

2. Try to answer the question: What are the obstacles we human beings face, both as individuals and as a community, as we try to be authentic? List everything that occurs to you.

3. Read the section on habits in this book (pages 79–82).

Session Five

Being Responsible

Scripture Passage: Acts 11:1–18
THE BAPTISM OF THE GENTILES EXPLAINED

Now the apostles and the believers who were in Judea heard that the Gentiles had also accepted the word of God. So when Peter went up to Jerusalem, the circumcised believers criticized him, saying, "Why did you go to uncircumcised men and eat with them?" Then Peter began to explain it to them, step by step, saying, "I was in the city of Joppa praying, and in a trance I saw a vision. There was something like a large sheet coming down from heaven, being lowered by its four corners; and it came close to me. As I looked at it closely I saw four-footed animals, beasts of prey, reptiles, and birds of the air. I also heard a voice saying to me, 'Get up, Peter; kill and eat.' But I replied, 'By no means, Lord; for nothing profane or unclean has ever entered my mouth.' But a second time the voice answered from heaven, 'What God has made clean, you must not call profane.' This happened three times; then everything was pulled up again to heaven. At that very moment three men, sent to me from Caesarea, arrived at the house where we were. The Spirit told me to go with them and not to make a distinction between them and us. These six brothers also accompanied me, and we entered the man's house. He told us how he had seen the angel standing in his house and saying, 'Send to Joppa and bring Simon, who is called Peter; he will give you a message by which you and your entire household will be saved.' And as I began to speak, the Holy Spirit fell upon them just as it had upon us at the beginning. And I remembered the word of the Lord, how he had said, 'John baptized with water, but you will be baptized with the Holy Spirit.' If then God gave them the same gift that he gave us when we believed in the Lord Jesus Christ, who was I that I could hinder God?" When they heard this, they were silenced. And they praised God, saying, "Then God has given even to the Gentiles the repentance that leads to life."

Habits

We have already talked about the fact that we human beings have to construct our own world, which is made up to a large degree of elements we receive from our environment: our parents, our family, our culture, and so on. This is normal; it is part of, and necessary to, being human. But this process contains a fundamental problem within it, which is that these things that we take in from our environment and incorporate into our own world are often faulty or incorrect.

A young woman had learned from her mother to always cut off the end of a roast before putting it into the roasting pan to cook it. She watched her mother do this for years, and when she grew up and cooked for her family, she did the same thing. But she began to wonder about this cooking rule, and one day asked her mother the reason for it. "I've always done it this way," her mother replied. "And that's how my mother did it. In fact, she still does. You know that." So the two of them went to the grandmother and asked her why she cut off the end of the roast before cooking it. "Why, I have to," the old woman told them. "I have a small roasting pan, and most roasts won't fit inside it unless I cut part of it off." "I never knew that," exclaimed the mother. "I just assumed it was what you were supposed to do, for the taste or something." "I thought everyone did it that way," said her daughter, "and my roasting pan is big, so I don't need to do it." "So is mine," said her mother. "All these years, I never needed to do it."

This is an example of a not-very-major mistake in one aspect of life: cooking. But mistakes can occur in all aspects of our lives and can have very serious consequences. Racism — in fact, any form of discrimination — is the result of distorted perceptions and beliefs being passed on through the generations. We all construct our world based at least in part on meanings that are in some way off the mark: inaccurate, incomplete, distorted.

Why do we do this? We actually don't have much choice in the matter. A basic reality of being human is that we have to live before we really know *how* to live. We have to function before we have had the experiences or resources to figure out how to do it for ourselves. We must accept things from other sources and use them, because we have nothing else. In fact, this is one of the primary jobs of parents: to provide their children with the tools they think necessary to function in the outside world. These tools are often the same ones they received from their own parents. This is how we pass on our faith and our values, but it may become a problem when the tools are flawed.

The other side of this is that one of the primary jobs of teenagers and young adults is to examine these tools — the values, ideas, and beliefs they were taught — and evaluate them and test them. They must decide what to keep, what to modify, and what to discard, as part of the ongoing process of constructing their own world. It's a developmental task. One big part of it is keeping the good elements, really appropriating them for ourselves.

The problem arises when we continue to keep these invalid elements as part of our world, even into adulthood. Furthermore, the longer they have been part of our world, and the more familiar they are, the more difficult they become to question or examine. It seems to us that they are not just part of our world but part of us. We cannot conceive of being without them. This is one way of defining habits: those thoughts, emotions, attitudes, and actions that we have practiced so much for so long a period of time that they are rooted within our subconscious and operate almost on their own.

Not all habits are negative, of course. But the very fact that habits are spontaneous ways of functioning means that we are not choosing them, evaluating them, or controlling them. We are following them. Thus, habits can hinder us greatly in our struggle to be authentic, to be faithful to the God-given dynamism of consciousness within us. Why? Because the very foundation of authenticity is mindfulness — consistently paying attention to what is happening both around us and inside us.

However, habits can also help us in our ongoing effort to be authentic. If we do something consistently, it will become a habit and we'll get better at it. In other words, practice makes perfect. But we have to decide consciously the good things that we want to practice and to what purpose, rather than operating on automatic pilot.

These are not new ideas. St. Paul exhorts the Christian community at Philippi: "Finally, beloved, whatever is true, whatever is honorable, whatever is just, whatever is pure, whatever is pleasing, whatever is commendable, if there is any excellence and if there is anything worthy of praise, think about these things" (Philippians 4:8). He is telling his readers — and us — that we need to be aware of, and monitor, what we focus on and how we think about things. The same principle holds true for action. We can try to become attentive to how we respond to things, and then use this awareness to guide our responses. We can choose how we act.

Work Pages for Session Five (pages 83–84)

Scripture Notes: Acts 11:1–18
THE BAPTISM OF THE GENTILES EXPLAINED

Session Notes

Preparation for Session Six

1. Read Acts 15:1–23, 28–29.

2. Redraw your horizons, on a separate sheet of paper.

3. Read "The Meaning of Community" (pages 88–92) in Session Six.

4. The Facilitator will present to the group an issue or problem currently facing your faith community. Think about this issue over the next week. What are your insights into it? Do you have any ideas for possible solutions? Write down your thoughts.

Session Six

Community

Scripture Passage: Acts 15:1-23, 28-29
A CHURCH DECISION

Then certain individuals came down from Judea and were teaching the brothers, "Unless you are circumcised according to the custom of Moses, you cannot be saved." And after Paul and Barnabas had no small dissension and debate with them, Paul and Barnabas and some of the others were appointed to go up to Jerusalem to discuss this question with the apostles and the elders. So they were sent on their way by the church, and as they passed through both Phoenicia and Samaria, they reported the conversion of the Gentiles, and brought great joy to all the believers. When they came to Jerusalem, they were welcomed by the church and the apostles and the elders, and they reported all that God had done with them. But some believers who belonged to the sect of the Pharisees stood up and said, "It is necessary for them to be circumcised and ordered to keep the law of Moses."

The apostles and the elders met together to consider this matter. After there had been much debate, Peter stood up and said to them, "My brothers, you know that in the early days God made a choice among you, that I should be the one through whom the Gentiles would hear the message of the good news and become believers. And God, who knows the human heart, testified to them by giving them the Holy Spirit, just as he did to us; and in cleansing their hearts by faith he has made no distinction between them and us. Now therefore why are you putting God to the test by placing on the neck of the disciples a yoke that neither our ancestors nor we have been able to bear? On the contrary, we believe that we will be saved through the grace of the Lord Jesus, just as they will."

After they finished speaking, James replied, "My brothers, listen to me. Simeon has related how God first looked favorably on the Gentiles, to take from among them a people for his name. . . . Therefore I have reached the decision that we should not trouble those Gentiles who are turning to God, but we should write to them to abstain only from things polluted by idols and from fornication and from whatever has been strangled and from blood. . . . "

Then the apostles and the elders, with the consent of the whole church, decided to choose men from among their members and to send them to Antioch with Paul and Barnabas. They sent Judas called Barsabbas, and Silas, leaders among the brothers, with the following letter: "The brothers, both the apostles and the elders, to the believers of Gentile origin in Antioch and Syria and Cilicia, greetings. Since we have heard that certain persons who have gone out from us, though with no instructions from us, have said things to disturb you and have unsettled your minds, we have decided unanimously to choose representatives and send them to you, along with our beloved Barnabas and Paul, who have risked their lives for the sake of our Lord Jesus Christ. We have therefore sent Judas and Silas, who themselves will tell you the same things by word of mouth. For it has seemed good to the Holy Spirit and to us to impose on you no further burden than these essentials: that you abstain from what has been sacrificed to idols and from blood and from what is strangled and from fornication. If you keep yourselves from these, you will do well. Farewell."

*The whole assembly kept silence, and listened to Barnabas
and Paul as they told of all the signs and wonders that God
had done through them among the Gentiles.*

The Meaning of Community

We all probably think we know what the word "community"
means. After all, we use it all the time, to refer to many things
and groups. We apply "community" to a small neighborhood
("It's a friendly community") and a large geographic area
("We have problems, being such a spread-out community").
We apply it to a group of people with a common characteristic who are living together ("This is a retirement community")
and a group of people linked by race or ethnicity, not necessarily living together (the African American community, the
Hispanic community). We also apply it to groups of people
with shared professional interests who are part of a larger society (the academic community, the scientific community) and
even to groups of nations with common interests or policies
(the international community).

Sociologist Robert Bellah says that we Americans use the
word very loosely. He prefers a stronger, and more focused,
meaning. In his book *Habits of the Heart,* he defines "community" as a group of people with a history (a past) and hope
for the future. Community members pass on that history and
their hope through storytelling. They also share certain activities — ritual, esthetic, ethical — that define the community
as a way of life. These activities almost always involve commitment. Community is interdependent and attempts to be
inclusive.

But when community means no more than the gathering of
the similar, Bellah says, it degenerates into a lifestyle enclave.

People who belong to such enclaves share some feature of private life — appearance, consumption, leisure activities — and one of its main goals is to enjoy being with those who "share one's lifestyle." Its members differentiate themselves from people with other lifestyles; enclaves tend to be segmental rather than inclusive. There is no interdependence and no shared history.

Most groups in America today, according to Bellah, have characteristics of both communities and lifestyle enclaves.

Interestingly, the Church seems to have known what true community is, long before sociology even became a discipline. The Church has a past: our roots in the Jewish tradition, the saving work of Jesus Christ, and the mission of the Church throughout the centuries since. The Church has hope for the future: we look for the redemption of the world, the resurrection of the dead, and life everlasting. The Church passes on its story: at every liturgy, we retell our history and proclaim our hope. The Church engages in activities that define who it is, and these activities require our commitment: our rituals, our evangelizing efforts, and our outreach. Finally, the Church tries to be inclusive: we welcome as members all those who wish to join.

The Church is a community because it recognizes — has always recognized — that we human beings are inherently interdependent. We are connected to each other in many ways, some of which are not readily apparent. What we do does affect other people, in often unexpected ways. This understanding runs directly counter to the notion of rugged individualism that is so much a part of American culture. Yet, if we look at some of the most important issues facing us today, we can perceive this underlying interdependence.

Acid rain, for instance, affects many countries in the world, and not only those that cause the acid rain. Winds can spread toxic chemicals far from their point of origin. In fact, many of our ecological problems have global consequences and will require global solutions. What we do in one place has repercussions elsewhere.

Economics works in much the same way. A falling birthrate in a European nation causes a labor shortage, so African workers are invited to fill the vacant jobs. These workers can then send money home to their families, leading to better lives for them and a stronger economy in that country. A stone thrown in a river causes ripples that touch land many miles away.

This is not a contemporary phenomenon. St. Paul understood interdependence, although he didn't call it that. In the First Letter to the Corinthians, he writes:

Indeed, the body does not consist of one member but of many. If the foot would say, "Because I am not a hand, I do not belong to the body," that would not make it any less a part of the body.... As it is, there are many members, yet one body. The eye cannot say to the hand, "I have no need of you," nor again the head to the feet, "I have no need of you...." If one member suffers, all suffer together with it; if one member is honored, all rejoice together with it. Now you are the body of Christ and individually members of it. (12:14–15, 20–21, 26–27)

This is not just a nice religious wish. Paul is describing reality; this is the way the world works. But we have a hard time seeing this. In the seventeenth century, Isaac Newton postulated the existence of a mechanical world that operates according to fixed rules. God, like a great clockmaker, started the world — this machine — running and then left it alone. We have treated our world and everything in it as a machine ever since, believing that the key to understanding it is to break it into its component parts. To understand how the human body works, then, we examine all its different organs and systems. To understand how radiation works, we look at the actions of its atoms and molecules. To understand how an organization works, we separate it into tasks and then study the workflow.

But Newton's view of the world has been displaced. Modern physics, specifically that branch of it called quantum mechanics, has made discoveries that radically change our understanding of how things work. Looking at what used to be called the building blocks of nature — the subatomic world — scientists now see that these most elementary pieces of life are not separate, isolated objects. They don't even exist as independent things. Rather, they are constantly changing, sometimes taking the form of particles, sometimes of waves, depending upon what they encounter. Relationship determines everything. One scientist has commented, "Relationships are all there is to reality."

This is the way the world works at its most fundamental level: not discrete, separate components but a web, a network of relationships, that is constantly in motion. Science writer Margaret Wheatley describes it as a "continuous dance of energy" and a "complex, never still, always weaving tapestry." What's more, scientists have realized that activity in this web is unpredictable, unlike Newton's deterministic model. The linear cause-and-effect with which we are familiar simply does not apply here.

In a fascinating development, experiments have proved that matter can be affected by seemingly unrelated events that occur elsewhere. It's "instantaneous action-at-a-distance." One experiment paired two electrons, meaning that they acted as one electron. They were then separated, to see if their relationship would survive at a distance. It did. They continued to act as one unified electron — showing that there exist invisible connections that stretch across time and space. Relationship is reality.

We are back to Paul's description of the Body of Christ. We are not islands, separated by oceans, but parts of a whole, linked together by invisible connections. We are a community.

Work Pages for Session Six (pages 93–94)

Scripture Notes: Acts 15:1–23, 28–29
A CHURCH DECISION

Session Notes

Select Bibliography

By Ignatius of Loyola

The Spiritual Exercises
The Autobiography of Ignatius

By Bernard Lonergan

Method in Theology. Toronto: University of Toronto Press, 1996 reprint. The structure of theological reflection: from research to pastoral theology.

A Second Collection. Toronto: University of Toronto Press, 1996 reprint. Essays, mostly on the transition from classicist to historical consciousness.

By Others

Bellah, Robert N., et al. *Habits of the Heart: Individualism and Commitment in American Life.* New York: Harper & Row, 1985.

Catechism of the Catholic Church. Liguori, Mo.: Liguori Publications, 1994.

Dunne, Tad. *Lonergan and Spirituality: Towards a Spiritual Integration.* Chicago: Loyola University Press, 1985. An exposition of Lonergan's theory of human interiority as an aid to understanding human spirituality.

Gregson, Vernon, ed. *The Desires of the Human Heart.* New York: Paulist Press, 1988. Articles by different authors on various dimensions of Lonergan's theology.

Hefling, Charles C. *Why Doctrines?* Cambridge, Mass.: Cowley, 1984. The religious significance of Christian doctrines.

Johnson, Luke Timothy. *Scripture and Discernment: Decision-Making in the Church.* Nashville: Abingdon Press, 1983; 1996. The processes of decision making and discernment in the Church of the New Testament.

Komonchak, Joseph A. *Foundations in Ecclesiology.* Supplementary issue of the Lonergan Workshop, vol. 11. Ed. Fred Lawrence. Boston: Boston College, 1995. The usefulness of Lonergan's categories and emphasis on self-appropriation for ecclesiology.

Liddy, Richard. *Transforming Light: Intellectual Conversion in the Early Lonergan.* Collegeville, Minn.: Liturgical Press, 1993. The sources and influences on Lonergan's own intellectual development.

Meyer, Ben F. *The Aims of Jesus.* San Jose, Calif.: Pickwick Publications, 2002. Lonergan and the interpretation of the Scriptures.

————. *Critical Realism and the New Testament.* Princeton Theological Monograph Series 17. Alison Park, Pa.: Pickwick Publications, 1989.

————. *The Early Christians: Their World Mission and Self-Discovery.* Wilmington, Del.: Michael Glazier, 1986.

————. *Reality and Illusion in New Testament Scholarship.* Collegeville, Minn.: Liturgical Press, 1994.

Stebbins, Michael. *The Divine Initiative: Grace, World-Order, and Human Freedom in the Early Writings of Bernard Lonergan.* Toronto: University of Toronto Press, 1995. Grace and providence in Lonergan's early writings.

Tarnas, Richard. *The Passion of the Western Mind.* New York: Ballantine Books, 1991. "The most lucid and concise presentation I have read of the grand lines of what every student should know about the history of Western thought. The writing is elegant and carries the reader with the momentum of a novel. . . . It is really a noble performance" (Joseph Campbell).

Tetlow, Joseph A. *Ignatius Loyola: Spiritual Exercises.* New York: Crossroad, 1992.

Wheatley, Margaret J. *Leadership and the New Science: Discovering Order in a Chaotic World.* 2d ed. San Francisco: Berrett-Koehler Publishers, 1999.